# The Abs Guide to I..... and Needlework

## A Simple, Handy Pocket Reference Guide with Step-by-Step Instructions Over 65 Photographs for Learning Over 15 Stitches with 7 FREE Patterns!

By

# Marie Stewart

AUTUMN LEAF
PUBLISHING PRESS

Design & Illustration by Olivia Butler

First Edition

# Table of Contents

# About the Author

Mari Stewart learned the craft of embroidery by watching her mother, Jacqueline, and grandmother, Harriet. She owes her love of fibers to them and her great aunt Marie Hardy who owned a dress shop in a small North Carolina town.

Embroidery was the gateway to lace, weaving, needlepoint, sewing, knitting, and many other ways to play with string.

Mari's work in environmental science and computer programming provided funds for her to follow her joy in the fiber arts.

String is an addiction she never hopes to quit and an enjoyment she hopes never to outgrow.

# Introduction

Embroidery is a skill both of the kitchen and of kings. With gold, silver, precious stones, and exotic materials, the ruling classes have announced their presence and their power.

Generations of girls and young women before us have made towels, sheets, tablecloths, and all the textiles they would need in their married life.

The Middle Ages saw the rise of professional embroidery guilds staffed by men practicing incredible art. Victorian women from all walks of life, from regal ladies in their finery to scullery maids in rags, would pick up needle and thread to decorate a cap or a pocket.

Even now samplers from great-great-aunts adorn the hallways of our homes.

Today you can see embroidery on fashion runways, on blouses and jeans, costumes, and even daily household items like napkins, baby clothes, and bookmarks.

The embellishment of clothing or items with needle and thread is almost as old as the concept of clothing.

The English word 'embroidery' comes to us from the Anglo-Norman root of 'enbrouder.'

In a way, the word is problematic because it encompasses such a massive collection of skills, materials, and forms.

The list of the forms of embroidery is extensive!

This list includes:

- Whitework
- Blackwork,
- Crewel
- Stumpwork
- Applique
- Hardangar
- Embroidered Lace
- Openwork
- Cross-stitch
- Needlepoint
- Candlewicking
- Opus anglicanum

The history of needlework goes back into the mists of time across every continent. It is very likely that if you can imagine something being composed with needle and thread, someone has already done it.

The topic of embroidery is a labyrinth where you can easily become lost until you know your way around.

In these pages, you will learn the basics of the vast world of embroidery. Some of the places where other skills branch off will be pointed out so that if you decide to pursue those avenues, you'll know where to look.

**Like mastering any other skill, you will need to practice. Share your successes and your failures. We've all had them both aplenty!**

One of the good things about embroidery is that it is one of the few skills where the practice is not only enjoyable, but you have a physical object to show off your hard work at the end of the process.

This isn't an exact science, so there's no harm done if you don't meet your idea of perfection. The goal of this guide is to leave you comfortable with your knowledge and new skill so that you can turn something ordinary into something special.

Embroidery is a method of remembrance. This is a skill that humans have practiced from the earliest civilizations.

Needle and thread are a part of our collective experience as humans. Embroidery is a skill we pass on to others, and the items we make tie families and friends together.

I wish you the very best in exploring this craft that so deftly ties together the future and the past.

# History

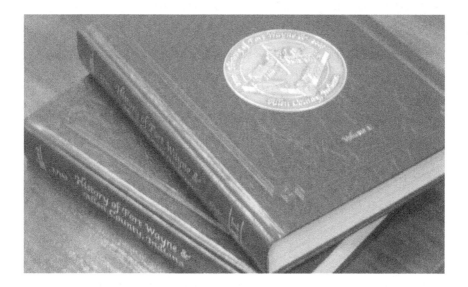

There are literally whole tomes written on embroidery.

Some books highlight specific works, a particular skill, or time period.

Other books examine the social and historical significance of embroidery and embellishment in the home and on clothing.

We can't guess exactly when embroidery began. Humans had "embroidery" as in decorating things by needle and thread before we even had writing.

For example, archeologists discovered letters from ancient Sumeria that describe the use of embroidery to adorn clothing over 5,000 years ago.

The Textile Research Center in Leiden provides this quote: "*The ancient Egyptians used a comparatively narrow range of decorative embroidery stitches. Identified to date, these are the blanket stitch, chain stitch, running stitch, satin stitch, seed stitch, stem stitch, and the twisted chain stitch.*"

The textile center also mentions the repair of worn textiles using various overcast stitches, darning type stitches, and couching. They dismiss these stitches as primarily functional, but in other cultures, these stitches hold a starring role in embroidery.

**Functional needlework is a different avenue of study. Pursuing it will lead you into an area of needlework called 'plain sewing.'**

The basic stitches mentioned in the quote seem to appear in early embroidery all over the world.

In the Americas, the beading traditions of the First Nations used a combination of back stitch and couching to support beads on the surface of the item or garment.

In South America, the Nazca culture decorated clothing and items with embroidery. Among the stitches they used were blanket stitch, chain, running stitches, and loop stitch.

The embroidery traditions of early China and Japan are vast and distinctly different from western Europe. But even these cultures employed the basic stitches of chain stitch, satin stitch, running stitch, seed stitch, and couching.

# Materials

The list of materials required for embroidery is very short.

What you will discover as you experiment with different threads and fabrics is the way the character of your work changes.

For example, the same pattern worked in chunky wool with a big needle on open canvas is going to look different from work done in single filament silk on a nearly transparent silk background.

Whether your taste runs to the rustic look of wool or the refined almost painted effect of delicate silken stitches, there are some fundamentals that underpin both ends of the embroidery spectrum.

## *Fabric Choices*

The first consideration is the material that you will use to support and display your work.

You can find examples from simple linen shirts, to velvet pillows, to woolen coats, to leather gloves, to canvas bags.

 **Most embroidery can be done without needing a special cloth described as "evenweave."**

There are very few rules outlining the fabric that you can use.

However, there are some guidelines to keep in mind while you are just starting out learning how to embroider.

## Woven fabric VS. Knitted one.

So, blue jeans are a yes (without Lycra), and T-shirts are a no.

A fabric that is evenly woven has the same number of threads going left to right as there are going up and down.

Some forms of embroidery depend on a background that is evenly woven. Needlepoint and counted cross stitch are two types of embroidery that rely on an evenly woven ground cloth.

## Use 18 to 30 Threads Per Inch.

There are specific fabrics that are conveniently labeled with the number of threads per inch in cotton and linen. They can be labeled 'needlepoint,' 'canvas,' 'aida,' and 'hardangar.'

In general, needlepoint and canvas have one thread crossing over one thread at every point. Aida and hardangar cloth have two threads crossing over two threads at every point.

Either type of fabric will work as long as you count each unit of 1 over 1 thread or 2 over 2 threads as a single unit.

## Consider the Surface

Does it have a shaggy surface? Does it have a velvet-like nap?

These types of fabric with a textured surface are best to skip in the beginning. When you're first learning embroidery techniques, a smooth surface without a nap or pattern is best.

Embroidery cloth is traditionally linen. Today it is usually linen or cotton. Wool and silk may also be used.

Some silks can prove to be slippery, depending on the finish of the fabric. (We'll discuss more on how to tame shiny silk in a later section.)

For counted designs, the higher number of threads to the inch (or centimeter) in the horizontal and vertical directions, the smaller your worked pattern will be. It will also be denser.

For children, an evenly striped cloth can be a good surface to start with to help them learn size and spacing.

Gingham with a small check also works well for this.

**Knitted items can be embroidered. To embroider on knits, you must have a good feel for not only for the stitches you can use but also for the knitting itself.**

The photo below demonstrates some of the different weights and weaves of cloth you can choose for your work.

From left to right, they are:

- ➢ A linen 1x1 canvas

- ➢ Lightweight cotton

- ➢ Medium weight linen that is almost but not perfectly even

- ➢ A fine evenweave embroidery cotton at 30 threads to the inch

The fabrics on the left and right ends are evenweave. This feature of their construction makes them appropriate for counted patterns.

The other two fabrics are not evenweave, so they are better suited to non-counted forms of embroidery.

# *Stability Assistance*

When learning, it is best to use a fabric that has a bit of stiffness to it. This makes putting it into your hoop and keeping it there easier.

If you find yourself with a fabric that insists on wilting, there are a few techniques you can employ to remedy this.

> ➢ If it is linen or cotton, give the cloth a pressing with a hot iron and a spritz of water. Sometimes that is all that is needed to allow you to get the fabric into your frame or hoop. Once the fabric is in the frame, the frame will do the work for you.

> ➢ If you need more stiffness, you can try a light spray of starch on the backside of the cloth. Let it dry completely before you handle it.

> ➢ If that's not enough, you can try iron-on featherweight interfacing. Test this on a sample of your cloth first.

But what if you just really want to use a lightweight silk fabric?

It may be the right color for your piece. Here is an example of how you can handle that situation.

I once found myself trying to embroider through a piece of silk that was nearly tissue weight because it was the perfect color.

 **The cloth needed more heft to it because the gold thread I was using was shredding the delicate silk.**

First, I tried a piece of iron on interfacing, but I didn't like what happened to the surface of the silk. It was time to go "old-school."

I found a piece of evenweave linen and lined my chosen silk with that, zig-zagging the edges together. Now the silk was supported.

The linen lining gave the hoop something to grip onto.

I had gained a very subtle counted mesh on the back of my silk, which proved invaluable for sewing the threads in straight lines.

# Thread

Just as there is a variety of materials for the ground, there is also a wide variety of threads you can employ to work your design.

The most common thread materials match the most common fabric materials. They are:

> Silk

> Cotton

➢ Wool

➢ Linen

There is no reason why you can't mix one fiber with another. Do be mindful that a really fine silken thread might get lost on a woolen fabric or a heavy cotton thread might be too heavy for a transparent silk background.

The fiber of the thread aside, an equally important feature is the weight of the thread and how it is finished. Both of these aspects will influence the final appearance of your work. The photos below demonstrate some of the differences you can find in thickness and finish of thread.

Silk is valued for the high gloss that it can obtain. You will notice that some threads can be unspun to get even finer single filaments.

Not every type of silk thread is meant to be divided. The violet thread in the photo is an example of a very fine thread meant to be used without parting the fibers.

The threads at the top of the photo in blue and brown are meant to be used as they are without being separated. This gives stitches made with them a larger, heavier feel.

The white thread near the bottom of the photo is called a 'perle' silk. This thread is meant to be used as is. The texture of the thread adds another layer of texture to the work.

The gold colored thread is called a 'floss.' It is made of six strands that are joined loosely. This allows the embroiderer to choose the weight of thread to use. One filament can be used for exceptionally fine work or use up to all six threads for a denser appearance.

Cotton is flexible, inexpensive, available in a world of colors, and a range of sizes and finishes. Cotton is perhaps the most common fiber used for embroidery today. It can come in a finish that is either glossy or matte.

Like silk, cotton floss can be parted to provide finer individual threads. It has the benefit of being accommodating of modern laundry practices.

**Wool was the first fiber. Even cultures that went on to master linen and silk have their foundations of clothing and embroidery in wool.**

A wool thread can provide a rustic look if you choose a heavy thread, or it can provide a cultured look from threads that are finer. You do not see the gloss from wool that you can obtain in silk or some types of cotton.

Linen is not commonly used for embroidery today, but it is used in some specific instances. Linen is traditionally used on towels and other white works such as sheets, napkins, runners, and table cloths.

It is used on embroidered and open-worked hems. It is hard wearing. Usually, linen thread is seen in white or natural, but it is available in other colors. It tends to have a crisp texture and comes in a variety of weights.

> **To pursue working with metal threads, you can start by looking for information on 'goldwork,' Opus Anglicanum, or shaded gold embroidery.**

Embroidery in gold and silver threads can be absolutely stunning. Using these materials is near the apex of the craft.

There are three major types of gold thread used in modern times:

- ➢ Lurex

- ➢ "Jap" gold

- ➢ Bullion

Of these three, learn with Lurex. It is synthetic and will be a kindness to your purse in the long run.

# Hoops or Frames

A primary concern in embroidery is the tension of your ground cloth as you form the stitches. Unless you are using a very stiff type of canvas for your background, you are going to need some help to keep the tension of your cloth even.

This is where embroidery hoops, embroidery stands, and frames come into play. Stands can be a substantial investment. For the purposes of this guide, we are going to limit the scope to using hoops.

## Hoops

The embroidery hoop is simply two concentric circles. One fits over the other, and the cloth is stretched gently over the inner hoop and held in place by the outer hoop.

To achieve this, the outer hoop usually has a screw on the outer edge to tighten it so it will grip the cloth better.

Most embroidery hoops you will find today are inexpensive and made of wood. In general, the less expensive hoops are primitive things that will pick at your cloth, catch your thread, and prove to be a nuisance. Not to mention giving you the odd splinter or two.

 **There is a workaround for these shortcomings of cheaper wooden hoops.**

You're going to need some twill tape or bias binding tape.

These photos show bias tape that has been ironed open along the center fold. The edges are left folded.

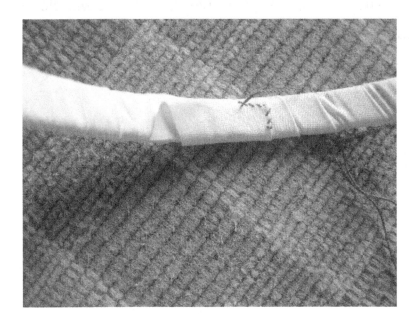

Wrap the bias tape around the inner hoop keeping it flat and covering the wood completely.

When you have covered the entire inner hoop, cut off the extra binding leaving about a ¼ inch.

Fold over the extra ¼ inch and then stitch the end of the binding into place on the inside face of the hoop.

**Don't use glue. You can't remove the binding if it is glued to the hoop.**

Open the screw on the outer hoop and fit the outer hoop over the inner hoop.

If your outer hoop is also catching threads, you can bind that one as well. Make sure you have ample give at the screw so you don't create an outer hoop that cannot fit over the inner hoop.

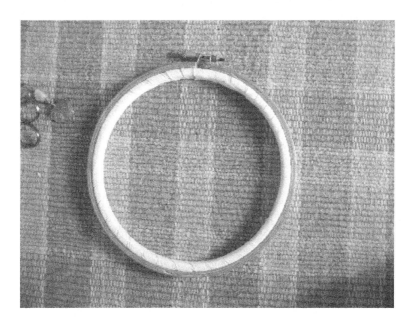

# *Frames*

The other way to support your work is by using an embroidery frame.

In a frame, you mount your cloth once for the entire project.

You do not need to reposition a frame as you make progress and it keeps you from having to handle a large hoop which can be heavy and cumbersome.

Stands for frames come in a variety of sizes and capabilities.

Usually, you will find that they are rectangular in shape. Oval is less common, but they do exist.

One variety of the rectangular frame can be resized.

This keeps your working area close in size to your project.

Frames are also good for very large projects. There is a type of frame called a 'scroll frame.'

This frame does exactly what it says.

A long piece of background cloth can be put on the ends of the frame.

Then, a spindle is used to store the fabric that is not being worked at one end.

As you move through the work, you release more of the cloth from the top and take up the slack at the other end of the frame by rolling the worked area onto a spindle located at the bottom.

# Incidental Tools

Other items you will need include:

## Scissors

You will need a good pair of small scissors with a very sharp nose.

If you are concerned about cutting things you shouldn't, you can look into a pair of small curved shears.

**Never bite your threads to cut them - use your scissors. The clean end will make threading a needle easier.**

They will help you keep the tips of your scissors away from your cloth and thread.

## Pencils or Chalk

You will need some way to transfer your design onto the cloth you are working with.

Make sure that whatever you use will wash out in case you change your mind or if a line isn't completely covered by stitches.

Your options include specific water-soluble pens as well as tailor's chalk.

## Transfer Paper

You will probably prefer to work out your design on a piece of paper and then use transfer paper to move it on to your working cloth.

An embroidery needle is usually a little longer than a typical sewing needle or a 'between' used for quilting.

Part of the reason for this is that the eye is a little longer to help pass bulky threads or flosses with multiple strands through. They are also sharper than those types of needles.

If you are working on canvas, in the case of needlepoint or similar practices, then your needle will be blunt. These are called tapestry needles.

The reason for the difference is that in embroidery on fabric, you need to pierce the cloth. When using canvas, you do not want to split a fiber that is forming part of your ground.

The most important thing is using a piece of fabric where you can practice your stitches and tension. It is your place to experiment.

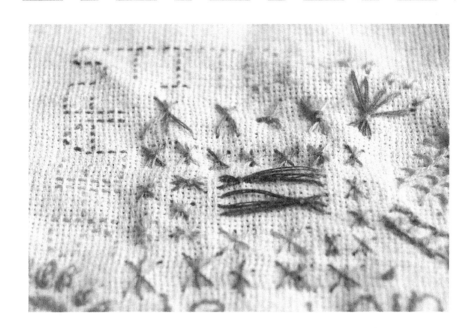

## Washing

You will need to decide whether to wash your fabric prior to starting your work.

> **Wash your hands before you pick up your needlework. Ensure that you don't have excess lotion or oils on your skin.**

For most fabrics, this means a gentle wash and then allowing it to air dry.

In general, it is best to wash your fabric once in the manner that you plan to launder it in the future before you begin.

Specialty cloths sold for embroidery in craft and hobby stores likely do not require washing. Do not wash canvas.

# *Cutting and Fray Control*

The next tasks are related - cutting a square piece of cloth and controlling any fraying that could happen.

The first thing to determine is how big does your piece of cloth need to be?

The answer may seem obvious.

It's as large as you need to hold your design, that will also allow it to fit easily into your frame or hoop.

Remember to leave a few inches around your design.

This space will be where your hoop grips.

If your frame is much smaller than your design, you can remove the cloth from the frame after each sitting and reorient it at the beginning of your next session.

There is a problem in this when you have to compress your already embroidered areas between the hoops.

 **It's better to have a big enough hoop before you begin. You don't want to squish your stitches!**

Now that you know the size of the cloth you need, your first instinct is probably to reach for the scissors.

Wait!

If you are using a counted design, then you first must be sure your fabric piece is square.

## Squaring Up

When we talk about square fabric, we are not talking about the shape you are planning to cut.

The object of squaring your cloth is to make sure that your cloth is not skewed as you begin.

Before you cut that fabric, make sure you are cutting it square.

**This is most important in counted designs.**

With most specialty fabrics for needlepoint and counted patterns, the work is done for you.

For creating non-counted designs, you can skip this step.

Square the end where the cloth was cut from the bolt first. With your cloth on a table, look at the edge.

Does it follow a single thread across from selvedge to selvedge?

If it does, you're good!

The "selvedge" means an edge produced on woven fabric during manufacturing that prevents it from unraveling.

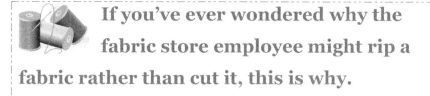 **If you've ever wondered why the fabric store employee might rip a fabric rather than cut it, this is why.**

Ideally, a rip will follow one thread; a cut will not.

The downside is that a rip can distort threads across the cloth.

If the end of your cloth does not follow just one thread, then this is how you make sure that all the threads are at 90 degrees to one another.

1. Find a thread running from side to side at the lowest point of the cut.

2. Gently lift that thread with a needle. Do you see how the fabric puckers to the left and right along that line? That is the 'straight' grain from side to side.

3. At this point, you can either gently pull the single thread from across your cloth, or you can run a pen down a ruler along that

puckered thread. The goal is to give you a line so that you know what is straight.

4. Measure from the cut end along the selvedge the length of cloth you need. It is best to use a ruler and not a tape measure because rulers don't stretch. Make sure the edge of your ruler is clean, so you don't put any marks on your cloth. This is also why you measure from the side along the selvedge and from the bottom edge.

5. Mark those distances, then tug gently on the thread at that point. It will cause your fabric to pucker a little.

6. Follow the thread that is under tension up and across until you find the place where they cross. Mark this point with a pin or an 'x' in something that will wash out.

Now, you have three options. You can either:

➤ Cut out your piece

➤ Mark the lines with a ruler and washable pencil or chalk and then cut

➤ Pull the vertical thread from your straight line near the cut end and then the horizontal thread from the selvedge

This will give you two guides for your cut that are aligned with the warp and weft of the cloth.

**Warp and weft are terms for the two basic components used in weaving to turn thread or yarn into fabric.**

Unless you are planning a hemstitch along an edge, or a piece of embroidery that goes straight up the middle like an arrow, you're probably going to be fine just cutting from the outer edge to your marked point.

If you want a little assurance, marking it with chalk or tailor's pencil first is quick and easy.

# The Perils of Fraying

You have just invested some of your time in making sure you have the right size of cloth you will need.

Take a little more time to make sure it doesn't unravel on you. There are several methods available to stop the edges of your cloth from fraying.

> ➢ Starch at just the edges to fix everything into place. If you aren't taking the hoop on and off, this method can help.

> ➢ Zigzag the edges with a sewing machine or serger.

> ➢ Overcast the edges.

> ➢ Use featherweight interfacing ironed on the edges only.

> ➢ Hem it.

> ➢ Masking tape or painting tape.

Using the tape method is possible, but not recommended.

Taping can leave you a messy, sticky edge. It will also make it hard to launder when you are finished.

# *Transferring the Design*

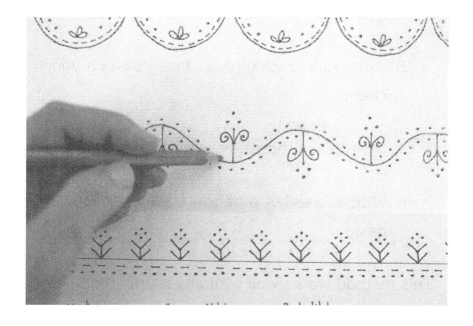

Getting your design onto the cloth is an essential step.

Before you put your cloth into your hoop, lay it flat on a smooth surface.

Transfer your chosen design onto it in one of the following manners.

## Transfer Paper

Using transfer paper keeps the design in the same orientation.

1. Place your cloth on a smooth surface.

2. Place your tracing paper face down on your cloth.

3. Next, place the paper with the design on top.

4. With a wheel or a pencil, trace over your design.

This method works well with any fabric.

## Pouncing

1. Draw your design on a piece of paper, then use a needle to pierce the lines with holes. Hold it up to the light to make sure you can see that you have not missed any lines.

2. Place the stencil you have made on top of the fabric. If you need to, you can tape it in place so that it does not wander.

3. Using a pounce pad, push powder chalk through the holes in the stencil. This will create a dotted outline of your design on the cloth. This keeps the design in the same orientation.

## A Light Box

Using a light box keeps the design in the same orientation.

1. With the design drawn in a dark line on paper, place your paper over a light source.

2. Place your fabric over the paper.

3. With the light coming from beneath the image, trace your design onto your cloth using pencil, chalk, or other water-soluble ink.

This method works best with light to medium weight cloth.

## Tracing

1. Draw your pattern on a piece of paper with a pencil.

2. Place it face down onto your cloth.

3. With a pencil or a pen, trace the image.

This flips the design around the vertical axis by 180°.

# Placing Your Hoop

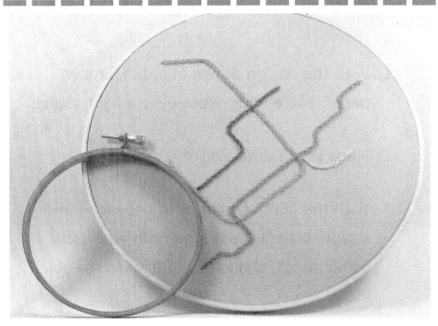

The exact tension you will prefer on your ground cloth is something you will have to experiment with to determine.

You want a taut surface to work. Make sure the cloth over the inner hoop is smooth.

**Leaving your work in the hoop under tension between sittings likely isn't going to cause a problem, but don't leave the cloth under tension for days on end.**

As you place the outer hoop, keep the tension on the fabric even. After you place the outer hoop over the cloth and inner hoop, you can stretch the fabric a little more.

Be careful that you do not distort the cloth. If the fabric is pulled unevenly, it can distort your work.

## *Organizing Your Thread*

Before you start to work, make sure you have the colors of thread or floss you will need.

It's best to have colors from the same dye lot so that you can avoid variations in your work.

Most prepared threads and flosses today are dyed under such controlled environments that variation between commercial lots is almost a relic of the past.

When you have all your skeins of floss, yarn, or thread that you will need, take a moment to organize them. If you neglect to do this step, you'll end up with hours of unnecessary work teasing your floss apart and untangling skeins.

There are several methods for taming your flosses and yarns. This guide is going to introduce you to two of them.

One method uses a dowel, a rack rail, or any similar rounded, smooth surface. The other method uses individual bobbins.

The first decision to make is, do you want to store your embroidery thread in one long piece or in individual lengths? The benefit to individual lengths is you can minimize tangling. The cost is that you might need to thread your needle more often.

 **If you opt for individual lengths, the rule of thumb is that you should never use a thread longer than from the tip of your middle finger to your elbow.**

As time goes on and you become more familiar with your own style, you may choose to work with longer or shorter lengths.

## The Dowel Method

The easiest way to store individual lengths of embroidery thread and to keep them accessible and knot free is to use the dowel method.

1. Gather all your cut lengths into an even bundle.

2. Lay them over your dowel or rod.

3. Bring the apex where the threads bend under the dowel.

4. Feed through the legs of the bundle one at a time.

5. Gently tighten the bundle against the dowel.

With this method, you can always retrieve another piece of thread easily. Place one or two fingers under a single thread and pull gently while stabilizing the dowel with the other hand.

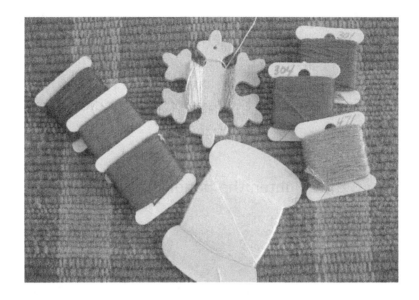

If you choose to keep your skeins in their original lengths, then the bobbin method of storage is preferred.

You will need one bobbin for each skein of floss or yarn. Bobbins are usually sold in your local hobby store. You can also make them.

A card that comes with a bit of yarn for a sweater can be reused or make small yarn holding cards by using a cut-up 3x5 card.

Bobbins can be plain or fancy. The most important features of the bobbin are that it has a space to place the name of the floss or a symbol and the number of the color.

 **Your bobbin choice should be non-abrasive to your floss. Inexpensive materials are good.**

Once you have chosen your bobbin and labeled it, the only thing left is to wind on the thread.

1. Start by removing the paper ends on the skein of floss.

2. Open up the skein until it forms a group of circles. There will be one end easier to unwind than the other, use that one.

3. Secure the end of your thread in one of the notches of your bobbin.

4. Gently wind the floss onto the bobbin. Try not to wind it tightly because that could cause it to stretch.

5. When you come to the end of the floss, tuck the end into the other notch in the bobbin.

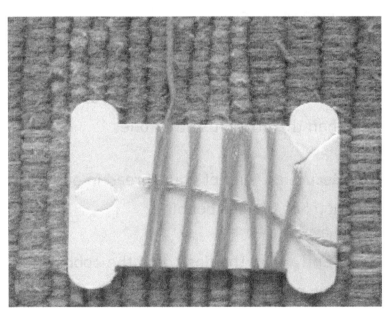

Having skeins wound on bobbins and then placed away in a case or folder where they will remain dry, dust free, and organized is a good investment.

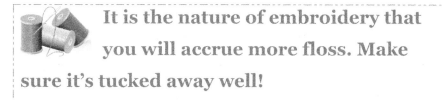 It is the nature of embroidery that you will accrue more floss. Make sure it's tucked away well!

Keeping your floss in this manner will prevent you from facing the dreaded disorganized "Box of Doom," where abused skeins go to multiply.

# Fundamentals

As this guide is for beginners, we're going to take a moment to talk about some items that people familiar with hand sewing might already know.

## Thread Tips

In embroidery, you can work with thread, yarn, or floss. Thread and yarn are not meant to be separated. Floss allows you to choose how many strands to use.

Here at the beginning, we're going to use a variety so you can really get a feel for how the thickness of thread can influence your product.

**The stitch you choose has an influence on what you do to your floss as you thread your needle.**

For outlining stitches and creating a solid border, using all 6 strands of floss is a good idea. For other stitches where you are trying to create a smooth, unbroken surface, it's better to use 2 or 3 strands of floss.

If you are using all 6 strands to create a border or line, just thread your needle.

If you are using 2 or 3 strands to help produce an even surface to fill in an area, then thread your needle and pass the full length of the strands through the eye. This will help them to un-twist and lay flatter on the surface of the cloth.

# *Threading a Needle*

This section may not be needed by everyone.

> Fifty years ago, it was a fair expectation that most people would have some experience with threading a needle. Today, this may not be the case.

Before introducing anything new, this is the time to master the first skill of working with a needle. The basics of threading a needle are fairly self-explanatory, but like almost any 'simple' task, there are things to keep in mind to make it easier.

One thing you might run into using multiple strands of floss is that they don't all want to go through the eye.

To solve this, you can try any combination of the following:

- Cut your end again to make it neater.

- Flatten the end between your fingers so all your strands fall in a single line.

- Try fewer strands.

- Try a slightly larger needle.

- Choose a needle with a large enough eye to accommodate your thread.

Some people insist that you hold the needle with your non-dominant hand and move the thread to and then through the needle's eye.

Almost an equal number of people claim that it is better to hold the thread in your non-dominant hand and to place the needle's eye over the end of the thread.

Both methods work.

The difference is that one is more visually oriented; the other is more tactile in nature.

**For embroidery and other multi-strand applications, I prefer the more tactile method.**

If you are having problems, there are two things you can do to help make the task easier: choose a needle with a larger eye or use a needle threader.

## Follow Your Fingers: The Tactile Method

1. Cut your thread or floss to the length you want. Cutting is important because it gives you a uniform edge at the end of the thread.

**Biting or pulling the thread to break it gives you a ragged edge with some fibers fraying, others bent, and others lagging behind.**

2. Dampen the end of your floss by moistening it between your lips.

3. Hold the thread between your thumb and index finger of your non-dominant hand.

4. Allow the barest tip of the thread to show between your fingers.

5. Using your thumb and index finger as a guide, slip the eye of the needle over the end of the thread.

The idea behind this method is to help the filaments form a straight edge, which in turn, allows you to slip the eye of the needle over the thread easily.

## Using a Tool

A needle threader used to be included in most needle packages. In case you have never seen one, a needle threader typically looks like a thin coin with a tiny wire loop attached.

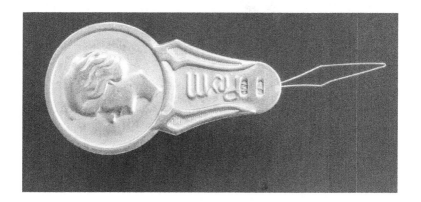

There are more modern types available, but they all do essentially the same thing.

To use a needle threading tool:

1. Place the wire loop through the eye of the needle. It's easier because unlike thread, it won't bend or deform.

2. Place your thread through the wire loop on the far side of your needle's eye.

3. Pull the loop back to you, and the thread is pulled through the eye with it.

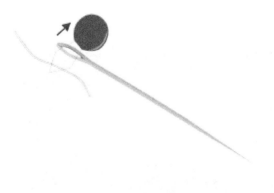

Once you have the thread or floss through the eye, make sure you have a long end and a short end.

> **Some people like to place a half knot at the eye to keep the needle from moving up and down the thread. This is not necessary.**

On the long tail of your embroidery thread, place a knot. It doesn't need to be elaborate. The knot just needs to keep your thread from slipping through the hole created by the needle.

## Starting and Finishing a Thread

To start a new thread, the first action with the needle is to bring it up from below through your cloth. Pull the thread gently until the knot lies flat against the fabric.

Finishing a thread is equally as easy. When you have made the last stitch you need, or you come to near the end of your thread, you end it.

To end a thread, stop on the backside of your work and form a half knot on the thread close to the fabric. You can use your finger to keep the knot from wandering away up the string.

Trim off the excess thread. Clear the eye of your needle if you need to and prepare a new thread.

Everything that happens between starting a thread and stopping a thread is what is presented in the next chapter.

What we have covered so far are the foundations that will allow you to develop your skill. From this point on, we'll talk about stitches, patterns, and how to finish your work.

**Embroidery is a pleasure. Pursue it because you enjoy it. Remember the ultimate goal here is your enjoyment, not perfection.**

Don't worry if your tension is a little off. That will come in time and practice.

Don't worry if the back side isn't neat. It isn't required to be.

Now you know all of the fundamental basics of starting an embroidery project. You're ready to practice some actual stitches!

# Stitches

There is a world of stitches waiting to be explored!

Stitches range from simple to ornate. Some stitches come with a rich history. Others have ties to alternate forms of art. Still, others can build on one another to form more elaborate patterns.

We'll start with the simplest form of each stitch and then demonstrate how it can be built upon. The focus will initially be on stitches used for outlining areas which may or may not be filled. The second group of stitches will concentrate on methods to fill spaces.

**The following stitches were chosen for a reason. What you will master with these stitches are the foundational skills that underpin every embroidery stitch.**

Even the most ornate stitches rely on a simple set of skills with the needle. You need to understand spacing, rhythm, and tension of a stitch.

➢ The simple running stitch is the first stitch to learn in order to master these skills.

➢ The back stitch epitomizes the action of the needle reappearing in a previous spot.

➢ The scroll stitch will be the introduction to manipulating your thread around the needle to form a knot.

➢ Chain stitch will help you understand how the formation of one stitch can lead to the formation of the next stitch.

71

Later, we will break the chain apart into individual loops. Each stitch is chosen to teach you a fundamental skill of needlework.

Once you have mastered these skills, you will be able to analyze and recreate almost any stitch.

## *Running Stitch*

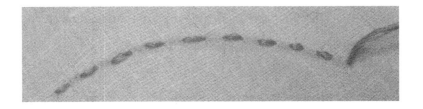

This is the simplest stitch. The needle passes up through the cloth and then down.

You usually see the stitch executed in evenly spaced intervals, but it isn't necessary.

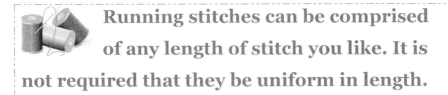 **Running stitches can be comprised of any length of stitch you like. It is not required that they be uniform in length.**

To make the stitch:

1. Come up from beneath your cloth at point 'A.'

2. Go down at point 'B.'

3. Repeat the action in the direction your stitch is traveling.

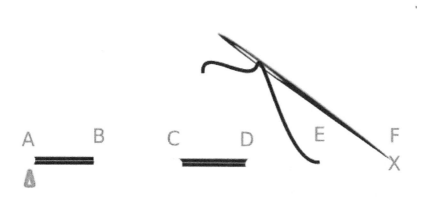

## *Holbein Stitch*

A common variation on the running stitch is called the Holbein stitch.

This stitch is commonly seen in the portraits painted by Hans Holbein in the 16th century.

In an outline, you simply stitch around the perimeter twice.

Every place that is left open on the first pass of running stitch is filled on the second pass.

When working in a line, you work a running stitch to the end of the line.

Work your way back to the point where you began, placing a stitch in every open space.

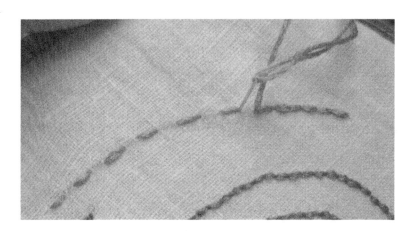

Using the example of a line above, you see how the returning pass uses the same points to form the stitches on the way back.

This fills in the spaces left empty by the first pass of running stitches.

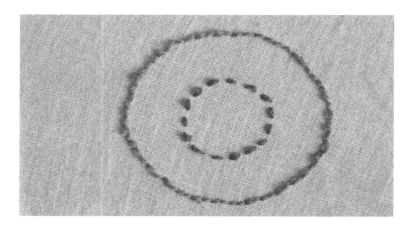

The inner circle is composed of a running stitch.

The outer circle is composed of a Holbein stitch.

The first pass of running stitches creates a broken line.

The second pass is made by placing stitches in the empty spaces resulting in a solid line.

# *Pattern Darning*

Running stitch, like most stitches, is not limited to being used for an outline. There is a practice in embroidery called 'pattern darning' which uses stitches like running, seed, and blanket stitches to fill in areas by combining the stitches in rows or patterns.

The photos show two examples of running stitch being used as a pattern.

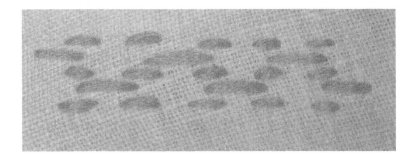

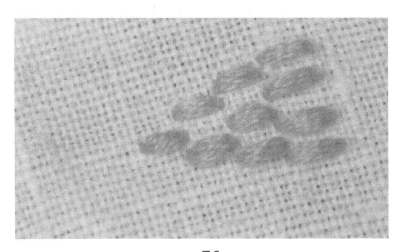

The number of patterns that can be made with a simple running stitch is limited only by your imagination. This is where your practice cloth can be invaluable as you experiment.

## *Back Stitch*

A close relative to the running stitch, the back stitch is used both to construct items as well as a decorative stitch.

You start the back stitch by passing the needle through the cloth in a short stitch.

That's the first stitch on the right in this photo.

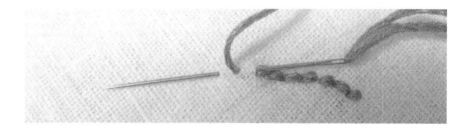

You first come up from below the cloth at point 'A' (the red arrow) then go down at point 'B.'

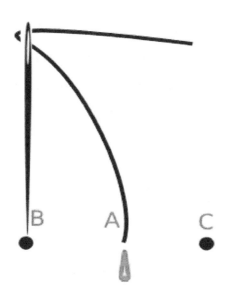

Your next stitch is twice the length of your first stitch.

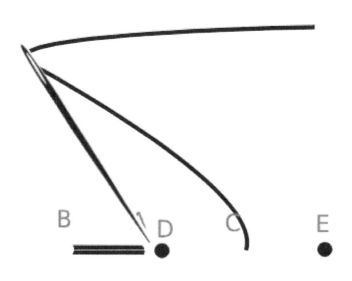

Your needle comes up at point 'C' as shown above. Then down at 'D.'

Now the pattern repeats itself. Notice how the stitch is formed in the direction opposite to the direction of travel.

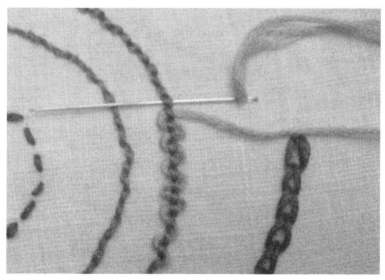

There are several variations on the back stitch that can take this plain functional stitch and imbue it with more interest.

Passing another thread back and forth through the stitches creates a serpentine pattern. It also makes an attractive and unusual border.

Whipping a thread around the stitches in a contrasting color creates a colorful border.

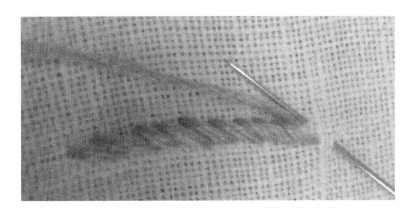

The whipped thread can help even out any 'wobbles' your line might be suffering.

# *Stem Stitch/Outline Stitch*

This stitch is commonly used to outline areas such as stems in floral themes.

Like the back stitch, it is formed by overlapping stitches.

The difference is, in this stitch, the stitches don't overlap one another directly.

Instead, they are obliquely related to one another.

# *Long Stem Stitch*

The same pattern used for the outline stitch is adapted for the long stem stitch.

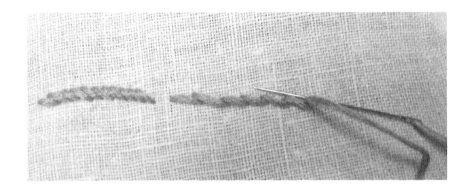

By increasing the distance between where you catch the cloth, you extend the stitch and make it less dense.

# *Scroll Stitch*

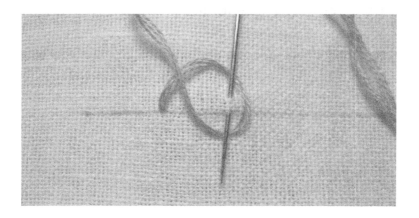

This stitch is lovely and rarely seen. It is called scroll stitch and is a take-off of the long stem stitch.

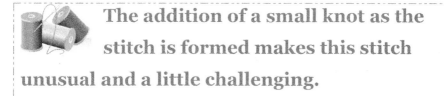 **The addition of a small knot as the stitch is formed makes this stitch unusual and a little challenging.**

Pass your needle under a few threads of the ground cloth.

Take the thread of your needle and wrap it clockwise under the needle; first under the back of the needle and then under the front.

Hold the thread out of the way as you draw the needle and thread through the fabric, tightening the knot near the cloth as you do.

# Chain Stitch

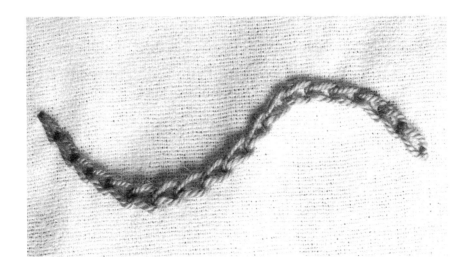

In the photo above is a line of chain stitch.

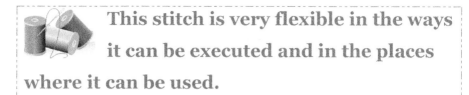

**This stitch is very flexible in the ways it can be executed and in the places where it can be used.**

Chain stitches can make a very dense border.

They can fill areas with something offering a bit more texture than the satin stitch.

As is illustrated above, even small changes in the size of the stitch, moving from larger to smaller can affect its appearance.

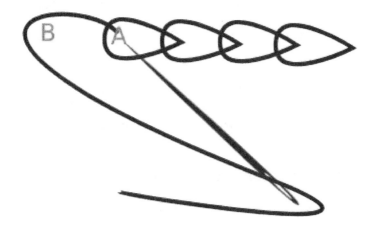

To execute chain stitch, the needle comes up at point 'A,' and it returns through to the wrong side of the cloth at the same point.

The tip of the needle comes up at point 'B,' and the thread forms a loop around it as it is drawn through the cloth.

 **Keeping a finger on the thread to keep it close to the cloth will help prevent snarls.**

To end your line of chains, secure the last loop by passing the needle to the back at point 'B' and placing a knot.

Variations on the chain stitch are almost infinite.

You can experiment by changing the length of your stitches.

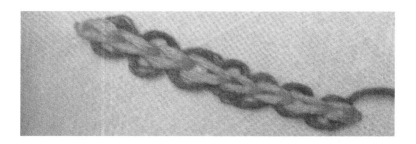

Other ideas include placing rows of chain stitch next to one another or weaving a thread through the loops of the chain.

Feel free to use your imagination and experiment!

# Blanket/Buttonhole Stitch

The last of the major outlining stitches is called the blanket stitch or buttonhole stitch.

It is formed in the same manner, whichever name you call it.

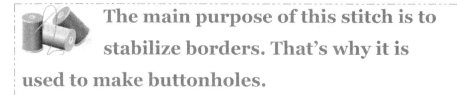

**The main purpose of this stitch is to stabilize borders. That's why it is used to make buttonholes.**

The stitch can be used to form a welt of thread along a raw edge. It also helps prevent fraying.

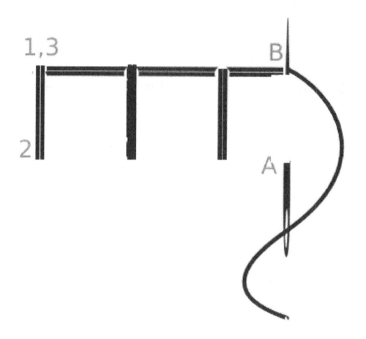

Once you have the stitch going, it is a simple movement from point 'A' to point 'B' by placing the thread behind the point of your needle.

That is what gives the right angle turn in the stitch.

Remember point 'B' can be the edge of your cloth.

Starting the blanket stitch is a little different than how the stitch progresses.

You need to start your thread near the top of your stitch.

That would be close to point '1' at the left side of the above drawing.

From there, you go directly to point 'A' and start your stitches.

That will make your first stitch start with a horizontal edge.

If you start the stitch at point '2,' then the leg of your first stitch will be at a slant to the right.

## Appliqué

The practice of sewing small decorative pieces of fabric onto clothes or items called appliqué. Blanket and buttonhole stitches bring us to this area of embroidery.

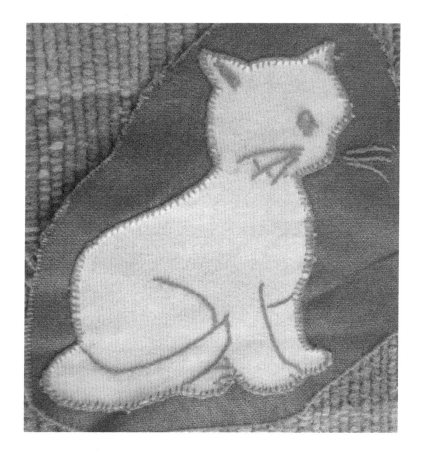

The image above is one example of the whimsy that was added to a child's romper.

A blanket stitch was used to "apply" the cat image to the piece. Hence the word "appliqué" meaning "to apply."

Appliqué is used in quilting, clothing, linens, bags, and other household items. The fabrics used can range from humble cotton that can stand frequent washing to silks that might have a place of pride on the wall.

It's another area of study that is rich with creativity.

## Filling Stitches

There are entire books written on the filling stitches for embroidery.

These stitches have names like

- ➢ Herringbone

- ➢ Jacob's Ladder

- ➢ Eyelet

- ➢ Cretan

- ➢ Tete-de-Bouef

**It is possible to spend every waking moment from now on learning new stitches. It's likely you still wouldn't know them all even after decades of work.**

As impressive and expansive as the collection of embroidery stitches is, it isn't magic. The motions you are learning with the outlining stitches are going to be echoed in the filling stitches.

In addition to that, most of the truly exotic stitches are made up of simpler motions executed in a specific pattern.

**The focus of this guide is on the fundamental elements that make up embroidery stitches.**

By learning the most rudimentary stitches, you'll be able to understand better new stitches you will find in the future.

# *Satin Stitch*

One of the most common stitches for filling an area is the satin stitch.

The goal for using this stitch is to create a smooth, uniform surface, ideally without any gaps between threads.

## Long and Short Stitch

This stitch is commonly employed when you need to shade an area. It allows the surface to be broken up while still conveying a refined finish.

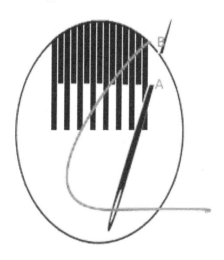

The example below was stitched with six strands of embroidery cotton. This gives a more textured surface.

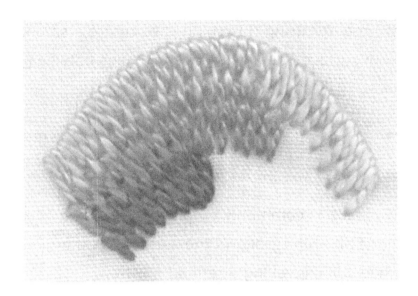

Working with fewer strands means you will use more stitches and create a smoother, more refined look.

This is the stitch to keep in mind when your area seems a little too large to cover with single strands of satin stitch.

## Detached Stitches

Every stitch we have explored until now has been a part of a line, a chain, or a series. What happens if you don't want a dense filling? This is where individual stitches can be used to create an airier feeling to your work.

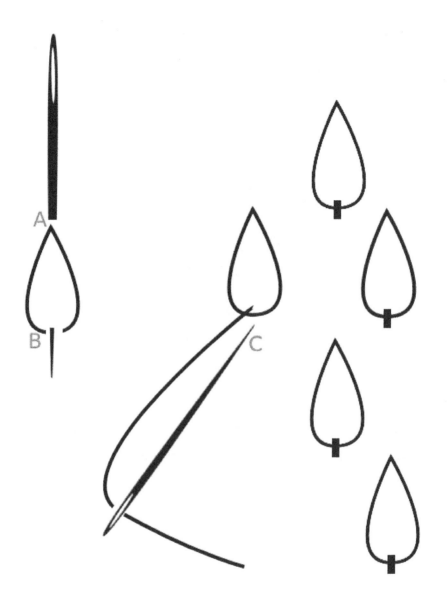

We have already looked at how running stitches varied in length can be used to fill a space. To use chain stitch, simply return the needle at point 'C' after you have made the loop.

Single chain stitches can also be used to speckle a background, represent seeds on strawberries, or define an area.

Putting several individual chain stitches together can form a flower. The stitch in this situation is called 'lazy daisy.'

## Cross Stitch

One of the most commonly used stitches in the United States is the cross stitch.

This simple filling stitch has spawned an entire industry. It is included in this guide because it is a staple of American embroidery culture.

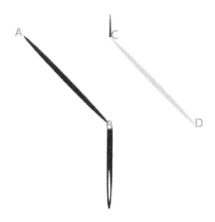

Starting at point 'A,' come up from below.

Make a stitch that ends at point 'B.'

Bring your needle back up at the top of the next stitch at point 'C.'

This may seem odd that you are creating a little row of slashes.

It is more efficient to form half the stitch on the trip out instead of trying to form the entire stitch as you go.

On the pass back from the end of your row or the second time around an outline, create the opposite facing slant. This completes your 'x.'

# Knots

There is one last stitch that you will frequently find in embroidery samplers and in patterns: the knot.

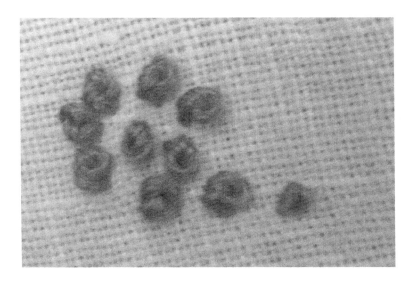

You've already learned one when practicing the scroll stitch.

Perhaps the most common knot in embroidery is the french knot.

 **Don't let the commonality of this type of knot keep you from investigating the myriad of knots that can be used in embroidery.**

Other types of knots include:

➢ Colonial knots

➢ Boullion

➢ Palestrino

➢ More exotic knots

One of the highlights of embroidery are the knots that can be employed to add a sense of three-dimensionality to the work.

The French knot is constructed of several movements. You will find that most knots use some combination of the following process.

# French Knot

Start by coming through your cloth from the backside at point 'A.'

Wrap the thread around your needle twice.

 It doesn't matter which way you wrap; just try to be consistent.

Then holding your thread, so you don't lose the wraps on the needle, insert the needle close to point 'A,' but not into point 'A.'

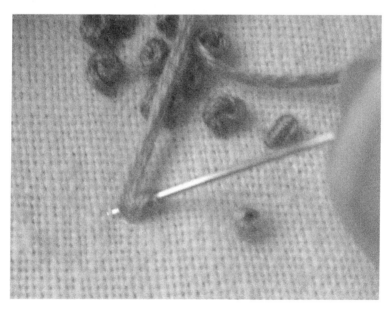

You should have 1 to 2 threads of your ground cloth for your knot to rest on. Keep a tiny amount of tension on your thread so that your wraps don't vanish.

> **You can even place a finger gently over the wraps as you pull the needle and thread through to keep the knot from traveling away from the fabric.**

# How to Care for Your Embroidered Pieces

You've finished something truly special! Take a moment to enjoy your work. You did this.

After some well-deserved congratulations, it is time to finish up the last tasks on this project.

1. Give your item a wash in mild soap to remove any hand oils it has accumulated while being worked.

2. Dry your item by placing it between two layers of towels or by laying it flat. You don't want it to stretch.

3. If your item needs to be pressed, make sure to use an iron at the minimum setting for the ground cloth.

**Use a piece of muslin over the top of your embroidery when you iron it. You don't want the tip of your iron catching any threads.**

Usually, embroidered pieces are small enough to wash in the sink. If you must wash it in the machine, place the item in a laundry bag for delicate items by itself. This will prevent buttons, clasps, zippers, and other clothing closures from catching in the stitches.

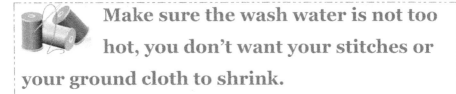 **Make sure the wash water is not too hot, you don't want your stitches or your ground cloth to shrink.**

If you are sure your laundry is only towels or linens without closures, hooks, or buttons, you can run your item through with them, but it can be risky.

Washed, dried, and pressed your work is now ready to wear, to use, or to give. Congratulations and onwards to the next idea.

# Practice Patterns

Here are some sample patterns to test your new found skills!

## Practice Pattern 1

The first practice pattern is a simple spider web. Try executing one in a running stitch, then another in the back stitch.

See how the change in the type of stitch changes the character of the work.

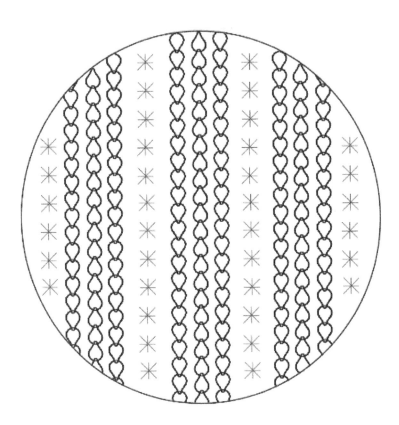

This pattern is all about using the running stitch and chain stitch.

Notice how the rows of chain travel in two different directions. The eyelets are made up of 8 running stitches that all share the same central hole.

This pattern can be worked on either counted or uncounted cloth.

## Practice Pattern 3

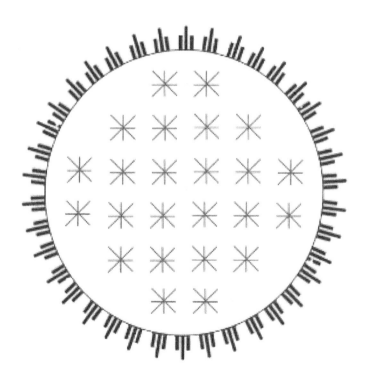

This pattern focuses on using the blanket stitch.

In this example, the connections between the stitches are on the inside of the circle. The legs vary in length to demonstrate that patterns can be formed with almost anything.

Try executing the pattern a second time, but now with the legs of the blanket stitch to the inside of the circle.

## *Practice Pattern 4*

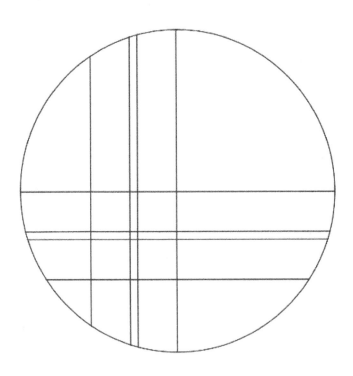

This pattern is for the specific practice of the satin stitch. The two broad stripes in both directions should be executed in the satin stitch.

Experiment with how the width of the stripe affects the ability of the stitch to cover the space evenly.

## Practice Pattern 5

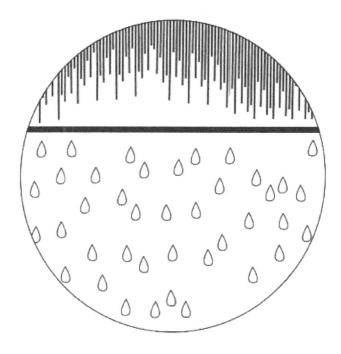

This pattern emphasizes the use of the long and short stitch. The individual seeds are single chain stitches.

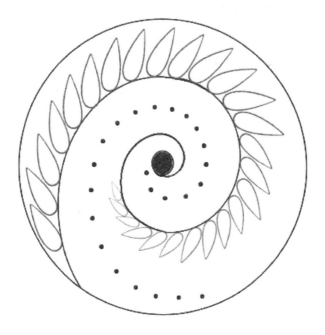

All those little dots are places for a french knot.

The stem is a great shape to practice stem stitch with.

The leaves are Holbein stitch or stem stitch.

That large dot in the center is a collection of french knots.

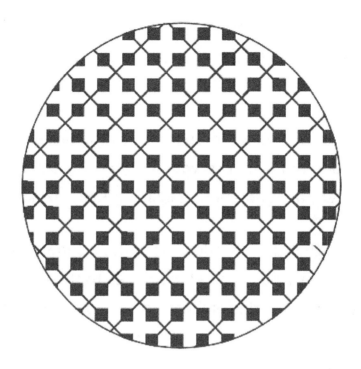

The last pattern is specifically for counted cloth.

You'll see the pattern repeats itself. It is made of running stitch and satin stitch.

# Conclusion

This guide to embroidery stitches is not exhaustive. There is a world full of stitches and designs out there to be explored.

From here, you are prepared with the basic knowledge that will help you decipher any stitch you find. There are endless possibilities! Keep exploring.

I hope that this introduction to the wonderful world of embroidery has opened your eyes to the many beautiful possibilities of what you could create. There is nothing more rewarding than crafting a piece with your own two hands.

If I have inspired you like my mother and grandmother inspired my love of needlework, would you please leave me a review wherever you purchased this book? Your feedback is extremely important to me, and I appreciate our mutual interest in embroidery.

Thank you again for taking part in my labor of love! Happy stitching!

Made in the USA
Monee, IL
16 January 2025

77077183R00066